FOREWORD

NINIAN CRICHTON STUART,
HEREDITARY KEEPER OF FALKLAND PALACE

Falkland is one of those rare places where centuries of human endeavour and creativity are woven into the natural beauty and built fabric of the environment. This is a vibrant place – in which the historic entities of palace, burgh and estate continue to act in vital relationship to each other. What excites me about living here is the vibrant sense of the place and its people who care for the legacy of our ancestors and are adding colourful and resilient layers for the future.

The origin of Falkland as a place name can be traced back to the 12th century, probably meaning 'hidden place', tucked in as it is beneath the Lomond Hills. This remains an essential quality of Falkland, with its hidden stories, paths and alleyways to discover, in surroundings ranging from heather moorland, rugged ravine and singing cascades to the outstanding 19th-century designed landscape of the House of Falkland and the 20th-century palace gardens. Whilst inside, inspiring craftsmanship in the palace and the House of Falkland provides so much to delight our senses. This was the place where kings, queens and courtiers paused and reflected on life. And it remains a place to take time out to discover nature and culture, then and now, inside and outside.

My great-grandfather, the 3rd Marquess of Bute, was primarily responsible for the quality of restoration and for adding new layers of craft and design that resonate deeply with its historic stones. His work at Falkland forms only part of his great architectural legacy that includes Cardiff Castle, Mount Stuart, Dumfries House and Glasgow University. Following the death of my grandfather, Lord Ninian, in the First World War and after playing their own part in the Second World War, my parents made this a vibrant family home, even if not the easiest to live in. Perhaps their greatest gift was to commission Percy Cane to design the splendid gardens we enjoy today and, once complete, to gift them for the enjoyment of the nation through the care of the National Trust for Scotland.

After many years as a community worker in run-down urban housing estates, I returned here in 1990 to play my part in revitalising a run-down rural estate and make it fit for purpose in a different age. In a place that once provided a feudal home and hunting lodge for the Stuart kings (High Stewards of Scotland before they laid claim to the crown for themselves) it has been a great joy to discover the relevance and potential of the old concept and practice of stewardship for the world today, locally and globally.

The role of Hereditary Keeper is an ancient office, with a range of archaic titles that go with it, such as Ranger of the Lomonds, Forester of Falkland and Steward of Fife. But for me the challenge of living out the role of Keeper and Steward is to act in a way that draws from the past, whilst seizing my moment in time to create a better place here with the community in a way that future generations will thank us for. In a decade of great change here in Scotland, that is a challenge … and this is a great place to meet it.

So I hope that you will discover some of Falkland's secrets, both in the layers of the past and in what is happening here today. And finally I hope you will learn something about the practice of stewardship and return home with some fire in your belly about what you can do to safeguard the future of things that matter most.

August 2015

HISTORY

A RENAISSANCE MASTERPIECE

The castle that preceded the palace was certainly here by 1337, and may have been begun in the previous century. Strategically placed at the meeting point of eastern Fife with the west route between the Firths of Forth and Tay, the castle belonged to the Earls of Fife. In the grounds you can see the remains of the circular tower, investigated and partially reconstructed by the 3rd Marquess of Bute in the 1890s.

King James I (reigned 1406–37) confiscated the Falkland estate in 1425 after the murder of his brother, suspecting Murdoch Stewart, the Earl of Fife, of involvement. In 1451 James II (reigned 1437–60) conferred the vacant earldom of Fife, together with Falkland Castle, on his wife, Mary of Gueldres (or Guilderland), and between 1453 and 1460 the king and queen made additions to the castle and adopted it as a royal residence. In 1458, James elevated the small rural village of Falkland to the status of Royal Burgh.

Falkland Palace owes most to two successive kings, James IV (1488–1513) and James V (1513–42), who between them created a Renaissance masterpiece with a strong French accent. James IV began a new palace here in 1501, the same year he began to extend the Palace of Holyroodhouse in Edinburgh; from this time until the late 17th century, the connection with the royal Stuarts determined the development of, first, the castle and, later, the palace. The community of Falkland also developed, to support the royal court when it was in residence.

James IV's new palace was envisaged as a quadrangle adjoining the existing courtyard of the castle. The first part to be built, by masons William Turnbull and John Brown, was the east range, which today survives as an impressive ruin. The north and south sides of the quadrangle were constructed between 1511 and 1513, with a hall range on the north and a chapel range on the south. The master mason here was William Thom, who had previously worked on Stirling Castle.

From top: remains of the ancient tower in the palace grounds; a heraldic Stuart lion on the burgh fountain; James IV (detail) (by an unknown artist, reproduced with permission from the Scottish National Portrait Gallery); and the ruined east range

Engraving by Hans Burgkmair (1473–1531) of the battle of Flodden, with James IV lying dead in the foreground

James IV was killed at the battle of Flodden Field in 1513, and the crown passed to his infant son James. Power struggles ensued during the years of the young king's minority: in the early summer of 1528 the 15-year-old James V escaped from virtual imprisonment at Falkland Palace disguised as a yeoman of the stables, riding under cover of darkness to the safety of his mother's care at Stirling Castle.

Work on the palace had halted with the death of James IV, but in 1528 William Barclay was appointed Keeper of the Palace and the following year John Scrymgeour, the King's Master of Works, oversaw the completion of the east range. The main programme of improvements began after James V's marriage to Madeleine de Valois, eldest daughter of Francis I of France, in 1537. The palace was important enough to be part of the marriage treaty: indeed, both Madeleine and James's second wife Marie de Guise were promised it as a 'jointure house' for their use in the event of their husband's death.

The King's Master of Works accounts from 1537 to 1541 have survived and show that the peak year for building at Falkland was 1539, when there were often more than 60 stonemasons on the site and the monthly building costs averaged £390. Some of the finest craftsmen of their day – including French stonemasons – built the spectacular entrance gatehouse, recast the interior of the east range and gave a new, strongly French character to the east and south ranges.

Stonemasons at work, an engraving from Jost Amman's Book of Trades, *published in 1568*

After Madeleine's death within months of their marriage, James speedily found a new bride, Marie de Guise. He and his new queen spent four nights at Falkland Palace following their wedding at St Andrews in July 1538. The building work continued throughout the royal visits, and the court must often have been living in the middle of a building site. After the completion of the project, James and his courtiers began to spend longer periods at Falkland, mostly from late August to late October, the main deer hunting season.

This double portrait of James V and his second wife, Marie de Guise, hangs in the Drawing Room of the palace. It is a copy of the famous painting in Hardwick Hall, Derbyshire (in the care of the National Trust), by an unknown artist (c1540)

LIFE AT COURT

A CENTRE OF CULTURE

The Scottish court of the 16th century was known throughout Europe for its encouragement of the arts and sciences. Falkland Palace, at the cutting edge of contemporary architecture, was a fitting setting for the vibrant court of James V, who cultivated scholars, poets, playwrights, composers and musicians. James himself played the lute and sang – though in a voice 'rawky and harske', according to a contemporary, Thomas Wood of St Andrews. Many French and Italian minstrels were employed at court; there was also a resident organist, viol players, trumpeters and drummers.

SIR DAVID LINDSAY OF THE MOUNT

The famous poet Sir David Lindsay of the Mount (c1486–1555), author of the still-performed play *Ayne Satyre of the Thrie Estates*, rose to prominence in James V's court, first as a herald then as Lord Lyon, King of Arms. His job was to proclaim the king's pronouncements to the people, and to carry out diplomatic missions on the Continent for James. He also fulfilled the role of court poet. His wife, Janet Douglas, was the royal seamstress.

Many passages in Lindsay's poetry bear witness to his closeness to James, especially during the king's childhood, when Lindsay was his main usher, or master of the household. In his poem *The Dreme*, written about 1526, Lindsay writes of James:

'When thou was young, I bore thee in mine arme
Full tenderlie, till thou began to gang
And in thy bed oft happit [wrapped] thee full warme
With lute in hand, syne sweetlie to thee sang.'

A later poem jokingly requests a loan of gold from the king, which Lindsay promises to repay

'When the Basse [the Bass Rock] and the Isle of May
Be sett upon the Mount Sinai;
When the lowmound beside Falkland
Be lifted to Northumberland'

… in other words, never!

Falkland Palace was primarily a royal retreat where the king and his courtiers would go out hunting and hawking nearly every day, beginning at 6 or 7 in the morning. They hunted both red and roe deer, wild boar, fox, rabbit, wildcat, marten and hare. The prey were bred and guarded by gamekeepers in the royal forest, and poaching was severely punished. The lower classes, who had to snare birds and smaller game outside the forest reserves, complained bitterly about this privilege.

James V kept a permanent staff of foresters, falconers, dog handlers and stablemen. The house occupied by the royal falconers still exists in Falkland, by Brunton Green. The king sent messengers to Spain, Denmark, France, England and Flanders to buy the best horses, and had a new stable block built at Falkland around 1530.

A hierarchy of servants cared for the court hunting dogs, which were kept outside the palace in kennels. Pages, or boy servants, would often sleep in the kennels with the dogs, to look after them and keep them from fighting. The warm doghouse would sometimes be much more comfortable than the servants' sleeping quarters indoors!

This copper alloy mount of a stag's head was found in 2007 at the north-west end of the Falkland 'trenches', an area on the estate that it is thought was used from the Middle Ages for the capture and sorting of deer for royal hunting grounds. Some historians believe this object may be a badge of office given to the men who moved the king's deer, to distinguish them from poachers

HAWKING

The ancient sport of hawking or falconry re-enacted at Falkland Palace

Hawking was a very prestigious pastime in the 16th century. In 1538 James Lindsey, the king's master falconer, was paid the handsome yearly fee of £66.13s.4d, and had seven more falconers working under him. Training a hawk was a painstaking process: at first the bird's eyelids would be sewn shut and it would be carried around on the trainer's arm, to accustom it to human presence.

Falconers from the Scottish court were dispatched to the Highlands to capture birds of prey and also every year to Holland, to bid for migrating hawks trapped there, which were regarded as the best.

Several words derived from falconry have passed into everyday English speech, such as the verb 'to hoodwink': the falconer would place a hood over the hawk's head in order to recover the captured prey from its talons.

The monogram IR for Iacobus Rex (King James) is a motif in the palace's painted ceilings

During the 1530s James's household accounts recorded 300–350 named staff: their own servants and their families, who they brought with them, would have swelled the numbers even further. The king's chamber, or personal, staff numbered just over two dozen, under the direction of the chamberlain and principal carver. They included stewards, carvers, cupbearers, ushers of the outer and inner chamber doors, yeomen, grooms and a barber, as well as someone to clean and lay fires. Some of the attendants would sleep on pallet beds in the king's bedchamber. The more ceremonial positions were given to nobles and other men of influence who would, for example, receive foreign dignitaries, or join the king in sporting or cultural pursuits.

A surviving document signed by James V shows his instructions to the master of the royal household, insisting that no one enters or leaves the court without proper authority – especially 'lads or vile boys'; that all servants should be decently housed, fed and clothed; and that their complaints about wages are dealt with speedily.

Dining tables, or boards, were mounted on trestles so that they could be easily dismantled and stacked against a wall after meals. Those on the upper tables would receive their dishes directly from the kitchen, while those of lower rank were expected to dine on their leftovers. A master cook was trusted with the king's life in an age that feared poisoning, and royal kitchen staff were obliged to take an oath of allegiance to their monarch.

The king, his household and his court were always on the move from one royal residence to another, often staying only a few nights and rarely more than a month. The most common itinerary was Edinburgh, Linlithgow, Stirling, Perth, Falkland and St Andrews. There is evidence that a 15-strong mule team was often used to transport the royal tapestries, coffers, tableware, clothing and portable beds. This could often require 12 carts for the king's goods and 12 for the queen's. En route the king may have broken his journey to rest at a noble house and give the servants time to prepare everything at his next stop: the host would be obliged to feed both the monarch and his retinue, often at punitive cost.

Food and drink at the Scottish court

Venison, stuck with cloves or sprigs of rosemary

Spit-roasted pork and lamb basted with butter and herbs

Roasted hare, stuffed with breadcrumbs, suet and herbs or spices

Hare and rabbit pie

Pigeons from the doocot – often the only fresh meat in winter

Peacocks, swans, quail, plovers, wild duck, herons, chickens and geese

Sparrows stewed in ale and herbs

Mince pies made with meat and fruit

Fish simmered and broiled in herbs and wine

Oatcakes baked on the griddle

Bread – white bread was reserved for the nobility

Spices such as ginger, pepper, nutmeg, mace, cloves, cinnamon, saffron, liquorice:

used to flavour and preserve food, considered good for the digestion,

and so costly that they were kept under lock and key

Ale (brewed from barley), beer (from hops), wine and whisky

THE END OF AN ERA

Fare weill Faulkland, the fortress of Fyfe
Thy polite park under the Lowmound law
Sum tyme in thee I led ane lustie lyfe,
The fallow deir to see them raike [move] in row

Sir David Lindsay, Complaint of the Papingo, *1530*

James V arrived with his courtiers on 6 December 1542 to spend Christmas at Falkland Palace. The catastrophic defeat of the Scottish troops by the English army at Solway Moss, the previous month, had plunged him into a deep depression. After visiting his current mistress at Tantallon – he sired at least seven illegitimate children, all by different mothers – James spent some days at Linlithgow Palace with his wife Marie, who was heavily pregnant. He then travelled on to Falkland Palace, immediately taking to his bed, probably suffering from dysentery or typhoid. Marie gave birth on 8 December to a girl – the future Mary, Queen of Scots. But the news failed to rally the king; he had hoped for a son, after the death of two infant boys, and is said to have commented bleakly: 'It cam wi' a lass and it will gang wi' a lass', fearing the imminent end of the Stuart dynasty that had begun with Marjorie, daughter of King Robert the Bruce. At midnight on 14 December, at the age of 30, James died, without ever having seen his baby daughter.

The king's body lay in state throughout December in the Chapel at Falkland, which was draped all in black. Sir David Lindsay of the Mount (see panel page 5) oversaw the trappings of the funeral and, later, the embellishing of the royal tomb. The king's corpse was embalmed, and the entrails removed to be buried separately. On 7 January 1543 it was escorted by a solemn procession of nobles to the ferry at Kinghorn and then across the Firth of Forth to Edinburgh, where James was buried in Holyrood Abbey.

James appears to have lost interest in the development of Falkland Palace after the death of his baby sons in 1541 and, with his death, building effectively came to an end, with the intended west range not even begun.

However his daughter Mary, who became Queen of Scots aged six days, enjoyed some of her happiest times at Falkland. She first visited at Easter 1562, and the Earl of Bothwell, who was then plotting against her, is said to have commented that the queen could easily be seized here, because every day she visited a nearby wood where stags were kept. Mary was an expert horse rider, and would have been introduced to hunting at an early age.

'OUR SOVERANE LADIE': MARY, QUEEN OF SCOTS (1542-87)

At the age of six, James V's daughter Mary was betrothed to Francis, the Dauphin of France, and sent to live at the French court: she married him in 1558 at the age of 15. Marie de Guise, her mother, governed Scotland in her absence, along with the Scottish nobles. When her mother died in 1561 Mary returned to Scotland to rule. Francis had died at the age of only 16, and Mary married Henry, Lord Darnley, in 1565 – for love rather than political strategy.

The Scottish parliament had established the Protestant religion in 1560, and Mary recognised this, though remaining a pious Catholic herself. John Knox, the leader of the reformed church in Scotland, famously denounced the young Catholic queen from the pulpit at St Giles' Cathedral, Edinburgh, warning that her arrival had plunged Scotland into 'sorow, dolour, darkness and all impietie'. England was governed by the Protestant Elizabeth I, Mary's cousin, but Mary was her heir, and many Roman Catholics thought Mary's claim to the English throne was better.

In 1566 the pregnant Mary's secretary, David Rizzio, was murdered by a group of Protestant nobles in her presence at the Palace of Holyroodhouse in Edinburgh. Darnley was implicated in the killing, perhaps motivated by jealousy, and Mary withdrew from him. She gave birth to her son James four months later. Darnley was assassinated in 1567 and three months later Mary shocked even her supporters by marrying the Earl of Bothwell, who had probably been involved in the murder.

Facing the opposition of Protestant nobles and a popular reaction against the Catholic Church, Mary was forced to abdicate the crown of Scotland in 1567 and her infant son became James VI of Scotland. She was imprisoned in Loch Leven Castle, then escaped, but was defeated at the battle of Langside. She fled to England to seek Elizabeth's protection, but was imprisoned for 19 years. Eventually, indicted for plotting the assassination of the English queen, Mary was beheaded on Elizabeth's orders at Fotheringay Castle, Northamptonshire, on 8 February 1587.

This posthumous portrait of Mary (English School) hangs in the Drawing Room. The French poet Pierre Ronsard wrote of the queen in 1561: 'The beauty of your face is forever imprinted on my heart'

A copy of Mary's death mask hangs above the entrance to the Queen's Room in the palace. A witness to her beheading reported: 'The executioners, kneeling, desired her Grace to forgive them ... who answered, "I forgive you with all my harte, for now, I hope, you shall make an end of all my troubles."'

James VI and his wife Anne of Denmark, English School. Both portraits hang in the Drawing Room of the palace

THE ONSET OF THE FALLOW YEARS

James, who became king of the Scots at the age of 13 months, knew little of his mother, the exiled Mary, and was brought up by nobles hostile to her. In 1603 he also inherited the throne of England and so united the crowns of the two kingdoms as James VI of Scotland and I of England. Like his mother, he also had happy associations with Falkland Palace, staying there frequently to hunt deer in the parks. In 1589 James conferred the palace on his consort, Anne of Denmark, and in 1595 he renewed Falkland's status as a Royal Burgh. But after his departure for London in 1603 he only once returned to Scotland and to Fife, in 1617. From this period the palace was administered by a series of Keepers.

In 1628 King Charles I commissioned improvements to the garden at Falkland, and spent five nights in the palace in 1633, during his visit to Scotland. All the royal and public rooms were especially decorated for this visit; only the Chapel ceiling still survives as a record of this.

Charles II spent some time in residence at Falkland Palace, following his coronation as King of Scotland at Scone in 1651. This was the last time a monarch stayed at the palace. In 1652, during the Commonwealth, it is recorded that timber was felled in the palace park on the orders of the Protector Oliver Cromwell, to build a fortress at Perth. In September 1654, as Cromwellian soldiers were ending their occupation of the palace, a fire thought to have been caused by an unattended cooking pot damaged the north range and the royal apartments in the east range.

The Stuarts' period as a royal dynasty ended with the death of Queen Anne in 1714. Falkland Palace therefore began a long period of decline from the late 17th to the early 19th century, halted by major restoration programmes of the 1890s and the 1950s and 1960s, which have added layers of great historic interest to the remains of the Renaissance palace.

Charles I after Daniel Mytens (c1590–before 1648): this portrait hangs in the Keeper's Bedroom

Charles II in garter robes by Circle of Sir Peter Lely (1618–80) in the palace's Drawing Room

This engraving by David Roberts (1796–1864), in the Keeper's Dressing Room, draws on the Romantic atmosphere of the palace during its years of decline

THE KEEPERS OF THE ROYAL PALACE

The office of Keeper of the Royal Palace, as it is known today, developed in the early 16th century, amalgamating the two already existing roles of keeper of the royal residence and keeper of the royal park. James V appointed the first of these keepers, Archibald, 6th Earl of Angus and second husband of Margaret Tudor, the widow of James IV.

The Bethunes of Creich, Fife landowners, held the keepership until 1602, when they were succeeded by the Murray or Stormont family. Sir David Murray was a great favourite of James VI, having helped to save him when his life was threatened by the Earl of Gowrie in the 1600 'Gowrie Conspiracy'. The Murrays were Keepers of the Palace and owners of the Falkland estate, a combination that has continued until the present day, though the extent of the estate has varied over time, and was frequently disputed.

In 1658 the 3rd Viscount Stormont passed his keepership to John, 2nd Earl of Atholl: again, the office was a reward for a family's loyalty to the Crown, this time during the Civil War years. The Atholls were Keepers until 1787, in an era where Scotland was ruled by sovereigns in London who had no interest in Falkland, enabling the Keepers to consolidate their position locally.

In 1787 John, 4th Duke of Atholl, sold the Falkland estate to Philip Skene, and for the next 40 years the land was owned by the Skene and Moncrieff families.

From the 18th century the owners of the Falkland estate lived in Nuthill House, which was demolished to build, between 1839 and 1844, the House of Falkland, which still commands the extensive designed landscape to the west of the burgh. John Bruce (1745–1826), a successful entrepreneur and prudent investor before becoming Professor of Logic at the University of Edinburgh, bought the estate in 1820. He was the first to begin to put the palace in a better state of repair. Bruce bequeathed the estate to his niece Margaret (1788–1869), who in 1828 married Onesiphorus Tyndall (1790–1855), and they continued to carry out repairs to the palace. Onesiphorus became a close friend of the 2nd Marquess of Bute while both were at school at Eton and, on the Marquess's death in 1848, became a trustee of his six-month-old heir and barrister agent for his estates.

IN·MEMORY
OF
ONESIPHORUS
TYNDALL·BRUCE
Esquire

The statue in the burgh of Onesiphorus Tyndall Bruce by Sir John Steell, the leading Scottish sculptor of his day (1804–91)

Architect William Burn's drawing of the House of Falkland, c1840

THE CRICHTON STUARTS

In 1887 John Patrick Crichton-Stuart, 3rd Marquess of Bute (1847–1900), became the owner of the Falkland estate and Keeper of the Royal Palace. A complex man – scholar, historian, archaeologist, romantic and mystic – Bute was one of the greatest patrons of art of his day. His many restoration projects included work at the ancient university of St Andrews during his Rectorship there, and at Cardiff Castle. Following a fire at the main family seat, Mount Stuart on the Isle of Bute, he commissioned the leading Scottish architect Robert Rowand Anderson to rebuild the house, transforming it into one of the most magnificent country houses of the late 19th century.

The restoration of Falkland Palace was the result of Lord Bute's partnership with another leading Arts & Crafts architect, John Kinross (1855–1931). The Marquess always ensured that there was a visible distinction between old and new work, even if the new work is often dazzling in quality. In Falkland Palace you can see outstanding examples of decorative metalwork and furniture produced in the Bute Workshops, established by the Marquess in Cardiff.

The Marquess of Bute's restoration work is remarkable in its attention to detail. Top left: ornamental hopper and drainpipe; top right and bottom: fine woodwork on the palace shutters

Michael and Barbara Crichton Stuart with their young family in the Drawing Room

John Patrick Crichton-Stuart, 3rd Marquess of Bute (1847–1900)

Lord Ninian Crichton-Stuart (1883–1915)

Michael Crichton Stuart (1915–81)

Ninian Crichton Stuart (1957–present)

On the 3rd Marquess's death in 1900, the Falkland estate and the title of Hereditary Keeper of Falkland Palace were inherited by his second son, Lord Ninian Crichton-Stuart. He was killed in the First World War and was succeeded in 1915 by his baby son, Michael, who later served with distinction in the Second World War and who afterwards, with his wife Barbara, made Falkland Palace their family home, letting the House of Falkland for use as a school.

Michael (1915–81) was a leading personality in the National Trust for Scotland and through his generosity the Trust was able to adopt the responsibilities of Deputy Keepership of the Palace and open it to the public. Employing the outstanding conservation architect Ian Lindsay, Michael carried out the reroofing of the south range, the renovation of the painted ceilings of the Chapel Royal, stone masonry repairs to the courtyard and High Street elevations of the palace, all with the guidance of Dr J S Richardson, Inspector of Ancient Monuments.

In 1981, on the death of his father, Ninian Crichton Stuart inherited the role of Keeper. Ninian returned to Falkland in 1990, and continues to use part of the palace as a family home.

TOUR OF THE PALACE

THE EXTERIOR

Falkland Palace is unusual for a royal palace in Britain, in that it stands right on the main village street. The south front on the High Street is dominated by the twin-towered gatehouse, completed in 1541. The towers are capped with conical 'prick roofs' which have a distinctly French look. The corbelled, or jutting, parapet is decorated with cable moulding, and the main roof of the gatehouse has characteristically Scottish 'crowsteps' – projections in the form of steps on the slopes of the gables. The central gargoyle above the entrance is carved in the form of a royal 'lyon' while the other gargoyles are in the shape of culverin guns (an early type of cannon). The gatehouse is strongly reminiscent of the north-west tower of the royal Palace of Holyroodhouse, Edinburgh: both were the work of the king's master mason John Brownhill.

Bullet marks can be seen on the front of the flanking towers. These may date from the attack by Francis Stuart, Earl of Bothwell, in an attempt to seize his cousin, James VI.

The three heraldic shields clasped by angel supporters are fine replacements of the time of the 3rd Marquess of Bute. Also of this period are the three beautiful carved and polychromed heraldic panels on the south front of the gatehouse. Colour may also originally have been used elsewhere on the façades of the palace – on the figure sculpture and roundels, for example.

The gate piers date from the late 19th century. Just in front of the left-hand pier is the provost's lamp, its glass panels displaying the burgh seal, granted in 1458, of a stag under an oak, symbolising Falkland's role as a hunting seat of the Stuart kings and queens. The Royal Burgh was abolished in 1974 as part of the reorganisation of local government, and the lamp was presented by the town council to the National Trust for Scotland.

The gatehouse is linked to the main south wing or chapel range, whose buttresses bear canopied niches with the remains of figures, probably of Christ and saints, carved by Peter Flemisman in 1539. The four large windows on the second floor mark the actual extent of the Chapel Royal. The south end of the 1501–8 east range, with its large windows probably of 1537–42, is also visible from the street.

Left: Fiona Allardyce and Karen Dundas of Scottish Wall Paintings Conservators during restoration work on the heraldic panels on the gatehouse. Above: the coats of arms of (from top) the Earls of Fife; Scotland; and the Stuarts of Bute

The Cross-House of 1529–32, which was restored by John Kinross for the 3rd Marquess of Bute in the 1890s, was intended as the beginning of the restoration of the whole of the east range. Michael Crichton Stuart wrote in 1972 that the 3rd Marquess had 'mercifully for the sake of future generations died before he could complete the restoration and roofing of the East Range'.

The interior façades of the east and south ranges, as remodelled in 1537–42, are widely admired as the most sophisticated architectural works of that date in Britain. On the east range, a distinctly French influence is shown in the column-buttresses supporting the walls, which may be by the French master masons Moses Martin or Nicolas Roy, and in the pairs of roundels above each first-floor window, containing portraits that seem to be of Roman emperors.

Right: the east range. Above: between each bay of the east range is a thin buttress inscribed IRSDG for 'Iacobus Rex Scotorum Dei Gratia' ('James by the Grace of God King of Scots'). Below: portrait bust on south range

The inner façade of the south range is even grander and more French in character with, as on the street side, six bays and two tiers of magnificent galleries, separated by elaborate buttresses. On either side of each window on the second floor is a roundel containing a portrait bust. On both sides of the south range the tall chimneys add to the drama of the skyline.

Right: This 1693 engraving of the Falkland Palace courtyard by John Slezer is thought to depict either the presentation of colours to the Scots Guards by Charles II on 22 July 1650 or Charles's return to Falkland after his Scottish coronation at Scone in January 1651. It shows the east range, then still intact

What was the palace made of?

Transporting timber: engraving by Jost Amman, 1568

The stone used in James V's remodelling of the palace – mostly ashlar or freestone, which was easily worked – was quarried locally on the Lomond Hills. It was carried downhill by sled and then by horse-drawn carts to the palace. Slates for the roofs came from Tealing in Angus and Dunkeld in Perthshire: they were transported on carts to Perth, ferried down the River Tay in flat-bottomed boats, unloaded at Lindores and then taken in carts to Falkland.

William Hill of Edinburgh supplied four great iron locks for the chambers of the tower and four great iron locks for the outer great doors, plus five smaller locks for the inner doors of the king's and queen's chambers. To safeguard royal security, locks and keys were changed frequently and very few household members were issued with keys to the royal apartments.

The oak beams for the early building came from Falkland Wood, but by the 1530s timber was being imported from Sweden, Denmark and the Baltic countries. The timbers were unloaded at Leith near Edinburgh, bound together with ropes, edged into the water at high tide, and towed across the Firth of Forth to Leven, where they were stacked, then cut to size and carted to Falkland.

Despite the expense of glass at the time, all the windows in the palace were glazed – even those in the kitchens, bakehouse and brewhouse.

The plaster used in the palace was imported, mainly from the gypsum beds of Montmartre, near Paris. Scots plasterers worked on the lower walls, while the more skilled French workmen plastered above the wooden beam that held the tapestries, since they knew how to make a smoother finish. After the plaster had dried, the walls above the tapestry hangings were normally painted: the surface was prepared with a white ground of chalk and size, then the design was outlined in black soot or powder, and the paint applied. The vivid pigments in the paint were ground from minerals and plants.

The Trust's Conservation Volunteers and garden staff help to clear vegetation from the well tower in 1994

In the early 1890s, soon after the 3rd Marquess of Bute became Keeper of the Palace, he began to delve into its fascinating history, digging several trenches to investigate the remains of the medieval castle that preceded the palace.

Although there are no known written accounts of Bute's investigations, he did leave a remarkable enormous plan showing what was found, which was rediscovered in 1994 rolled up in an attic. It shows Bute's trenches clearly, and in dark red where he found walls associated with Falkland Castle and with the house that was built over it and was known to exist in the 17th century.

Of particular interest are the foundations in the north-east corner of the castle of a round tower with a well in the middle. It has been associated with the imprisonment and alleged murder of the Duke of Rothesay in 1401, but the string course (horizontal band) in the stone footings that Bute discovered show that it was built much earlier, in the 13th century. Archaeological investigations in 1994 of this tower and an adjacent D-shaped tower revealed the flat patio-like surface that you see today, along with a carved well-head of possible 17th-century date. Parts of the foundations were made of red sandstone – evidence that Bute had been there before, leaving this layer to mark the boundary between the original structure and the new. This showed that the 'patio' was entirely the result of Bute's restoration, and had little to do with the flooring of the medieval castle – which had probably been substantially robbed of its stone, for re-use in later buildings.

Lord Bute's sandstone boundary – included at considerable extra cost – has helped modern archaeologists to quickly understand what had been done, guiding the conservation of the remains over a century later. The principle of distinguishing between old and new work during conservation of historic buildings is now considered to be best practice

THE INTERIOR

The room opposite Reception is believed to have been a guardroom when the Stuart monarchs stayed at Falkland, for from here access could be gained to all areas of the palace via the basement. Later, during the keepership of the 3rd Marquess of Bute and the Crichton-Stuarts, the room was used as servants' quarters along with the current reception area.

Visitors leave this room through the door to the right, taking the turnpike stair up to the next floor.

From top: detail of carving on the bed; the inscription on the frieze round the bed reads: 'Fere God His Will Obay For To Heven It Is The Waie'

Lord Bute's profile, showing him hooded like a monk in the romantic robes designed for him as Rector of the University of St Andrews, is carved on the door leading to the Dressing Room

The 'bones' of this room date from the 1890s restoration, including the painted ceiling and the window shutters. The spectacular tester bed was brought here by Michael Crichton Stuart from Rossie Priory, Perthshire. Dated 1618, it is said to have been made in Aberdeen for James VI, and is a superb example of rich carving and complex inlay work in fruitwoods and ebony.

In one corner is a richly carved cupboard which incorporates pieces dated 1638 and containing the names Alexander and Eliner Hodgson: these may have come from a marriage chest. The table and the two fine chairs are 17th-century in manner, but created during the 1890s restoration and, like the shutters and much other furniture in the palace, probably made at the Bute Workshops in Cardiff. The mirror over the fireplace is in the Charles II style but also made in the late 19th century.

The wash-hand basin here is edged with predominantly red marble – probably Welsh – and encased in an outer octagonal wooden bowl with linenfold panelling, which may be a reference to the weaving industry which at one time flourished in Falkland. The design of the ceiling, painted by Andrew Lyons in 1895, incorporates the Crichton Stuart family motto *'Nobilis est ira leonis'* ('Noble is the wrath of the lion') and the motto on the royal coat of arms of Scotland, *'Nemo me impune lacessit'* ('No one provokes me with impunity').

From the Keeper's Bedroom the visitor returns to the floor below.

The superb table and set of chairs, along with a number of other items in the room, were made at the Bute Workshops for the House of Falkland, but have been displayed here since the palace opened to visitors.

The carved profiles of the Bute children on the cupboard in this room, dated 1895, show Margaret, later the first woman to achieve a Master Mariner's Certificate, John, who became the 4th Marquess, Ninian, who inherited the Falkland estate, and Colum, who inherited Pluscarden Abbey and estate

The late 19th-century Chinese figures of 'the Eight Immortals' were originally umbrella stands, but converted by Barbara Crichton Stuart into table-lamp stands to protect their fragility

The Keeper's family use this room in the winter months, and on display are many objects and memorabilia associated with the Crichton Stuarts. Again, much of the restoration of this room was carried out in 1895–6: note the date of 1896 on the shutters. The painted decoration in the window alcove, the richly carved wainscoting (wall panelling), the large rectangular panels on the ceiling with the coats of arms of the Hereditary Keepers, together with the royal arms, all are of the 1890s, the joinery being by the Edinburgh firm of Scott Morton.

The other furniture dates from the 17th century, as does the stumpwork (raised embroidery) mirror frame, which was remounted by Helen Sutherland in the early 1990s. Barbara Crichton Stuart had the green hessian wall-hangings above the wall panelling dyed to match the carpet in the early 1950s.

Stuart portraits in the Drawing Room

The striking portraits in this room depict members of the royal Stuart family who were so closely identified with the palace. James VI (right) was painted by Alonso Sanchez Coello in 1586. The portrait of James Francis Edward Stuart and his sister Marie-Louise, by Nicolas de Largillière, *c*1700 (below), is a copy of one in the National Portrait Gallery, London. The young Prince James, then in exile in France, was later to become the focus of the Jacobite claim to the British throne.

Other Stuarts portrayed here include James V and his second wife, Marie de Guise and Lorraine; Mary, Queen of Scots; James VI's wife, Anne of Denmark; and James VI's grandson, Charles II, both as a young and old man.

Michael Crichton Stuart, painted in this room by his daughter, Frances

Beyond the Drawing Room, the Library is one of the Keeper's private apartments but can often be viewed from the door. The bookcases, many of the books and the massive sofa were brought here by Michael and Barbara Crichton Stuart, the present Keeper's parents, from the House of Falkland. Michael Crichton Stuart commissioned Alec Thom of St Andrews to design and construct a 'secret' door giving access to a small room off the library. The door was painted with false shelves, and spines from old leather-bound volumes were glued to it to make it look like part of the surrounding bookcase. The 'secret room' was a bedroom during Michael and Barbara's residence, but is now used as an office.

Returning to the Drawing Room, the visitor enters the Chapel Royal through a short corridor, which still contains the 'dumb waiter' and a speaking tube, in service during the late 19th century when the Drawing Room was used as a dining room.

The Chapel Royal was begun by James IV but remained unfinished at the time of his death at the battle of Flodden in 1513. Under his successor, James V, the Chapel was completed and consecrated, and a door knocked through to the Gallery next to the Chapel, a new addition to the palace. James commissioned Richard Stewart, who had worked at the Palace of Holyroodhouse, to make the oak wall panels and the wooden panelled ceiling which, at its eastern end, forms a canopy of honour over the altar. The centre panel is painted in the blue-and-white colours of the royal St Andrew's Cross, as in the Queen's Oratory at Holyroodhouse. The pendant escutcheon (shield) in the middle of the ceiling bears the arms of Charles I.

The ante-chapel is separated from the Chapel proper by an openwork screen of turned oak balusters, no two of which are exactly alike, also made in the early 16th century.

This signature carved on the wall of the Chapel Royal, behind the pulpit, is thought to be of Mary, Queen of Scots. Below: the altar rail

This image of the Virgin, to the right of the Chapel exit, was made by Polish soldiers stationed at Falkland during the Second World War, from metal bullet casings and corned beef tins. It is a copy of the Madonna of Ostrobrama in Vilnius, Lithuania

After James V's untimely death, his body lay here from 14 December 1542 until 7 January 1543, and the Chapel was draped in black. His daughter Mary, Queen of Scots, worshipped regularly here: on Maundy Thursday 1562 she washed the feet of 19 virgins in the Chapel, one for each year of her reign, and presented them with a length of blue linen cloth.

The painted decoration of the ceiling and the frieze on the north side of the Chapel date from the time of Charles I. The ceiling incorporates Stuart and Tudor royal badges and the initials of Charles I (CR for *Carolus Rex*), Henrietta Maria, Charles's wife (MR for *Maria Regina*) and Charles, Prince of Wales, their son (CP for *Carolus Princeps*). The frieze on the north side dates from 1633, when the Chapel was redecorated to mark the coronation of Charles I as King of Scots, and incorporates his monogram again, with those of his queen and heir on either side. The frieze is of wood, painted with latticed windows to balance the real ones on the south side of the Chapel.

The frieze on the south side dates from Lord Bute's restoration. Set into the windows are panels by Lord Bute's favourite stained glass artist, Horatio Walter Lonsdale, showing the heraldic badges of Scottish kings and queens associated with Falkland Palace.

The royal pew on the north wall is a reconstruction, commissioned by Lord Bute, and incorporating pieces of decorative woodwork from the original 16th-century pew, which Bute found during excavations of the palace cellars.

On the north wall of the Chapel hang Flemish tapestries of *c*1600 depicting scenes from the biblical story of Joseph and Benjamin. The tapestries hang from a painted wooden moulded frieze whose Latin inscriptions are from Psalm 21 and read, in translation, 'For the king trusteth in the Lord and through the mercy of the most high he shall not be moved. Be thou exalted Lord in thine own strength, so will we sing and praise thy power'. This, together with the simple oak panelling below the tapestries, is by the architect W Schomberg Scott, who was commissioned by the Trust after it took responsibility for the palace in 1952. Also by him is the altar rail of 1965, commissioned by Michael Crichton Stuart, which displays the symbols of the 12 apostles, the thistles of Scotland and the acorns and oak leaves of the House of Stuart.

The altar, by leading Arts & Crafts architect Robert Weir Schultz, was commissioned in the early 20th century by the Dowager Marchioness of Bute and her son Lord Ninian Crichton-Stuart, who wanted to revive the Chapel after two-and-a-half centuries of disuse. In the post-Second World War period Colonel Elwes, a Catholic architect and decorator, designed the tabernacle and setting of the altar, reusing rich hangings from the House of Falkland. The specially designed candlesticks bear shields decorated with the Scots thistle, the French fleur-de-lys and the English-Welsh Tudor rose.

A final touch was added in 1978–9 with no fewer than 140 new kneelers designed by W Schomberg Scott and embroidered at the initiative of June Baxter by the Trust's East Fife Members' Centre and the canvas embroidery class at Hill of Tarvit, in Fife.

This Gallery provided access from the royal apartments to the Chapel. Almost the whole of the south wall is hung with a series of 17th-century Flemish tapestries, showing idyllic hunting scenes. They were acquired by Lord Ninian in 1906 and hung at first in the Chapel.

The Stuart monarchs would take their tapestries with them when they travelled, to hang wherever they were staying next: a Master of Tapestries was responsible for taking care of them and for nailing them to the battens just as the king entered the courtyard – a nerve-wracking task!

The four court cupboards between the large windows were made in the 1890s by John Small, at Lord Bute's workshops in Cardiff, working from 17th-century pattern books.

From top: details of the Gallery tapestries from west to east: a waterfall, with a huntsman shooting birds; a lion savaging a bird; a lion with a bird in its mouth. All five tapestries include delightful details such as the pair of rabbits (bottom)

The fine portraits in the Gallery include those of Charlotte Jane Windsor, Viscountess Mountstuart and Baroness Cardiff, after George Romney, 1785; and Charles I, after Sir Anthony van Dyck (1599–1641), one of the iconic royal images of 17th-century Britain

Lord Ninian Crichton-Stuart and his mother, the 3rd Marchioness of Bute, in mourning dress, are shown in this 1904 portrait in the Old Library

This unusual room, also known as the Edwardian Library, was used by Michael Crichton Stuart as his study. It dates entirely from Lord Bute's restorations. The whole room is lined in pine. The tunnel-vaulted ceiling was decorated by Thomas Bonnar, junior, who also painted the *trompe l'oeil* skirting board and window on the north side to balance the real one on the south side.

Over the fireplace is a fine royal arms of Charles II, painted on wooden panels. It dates from *c*1660 and was purchased by the Trust, with the aid of a grant from the Local Museums Purchase Fund, in 1982. Several pieces of furniture, for example the table along the east wall, were made in the 1890s for the 3rd Marquess of Bute, whose photograph, with his characteristic beard, is among the family collection on the table.

Descending from here to the basement, the visitor finds the Bakehouse. This room is also lit by a single high window towards the High Street. In one corner stands the 17th-century bread oven, which would have been constantly alight while the royal household was in residence, producing hundreds of loaves every day. The room contains a notable long work-table, a chest for storing flour and a dough box for making bread (right).

Leaving the south wing by the great stair at first-floor level, the visitor emerges into the open air in the ruined east wing, once part of the state rooms of the royal palace. It is thought that the rooms here were the king's guard room, the presence chamber, the king's bedroom, a withdrawing room and the eating room at the north end. The east wing was damaged by fire in 1654.

Accessed at this level is the Cross-House, built by James IV, which now houses a fascinating late 20th-century interpretation of two royal bedchambers, the King's Room and the Queen's Room, the queen being Mary, Queen of Scots.

At the top of the stairs outside the Old Library is a fine ironwork screen (left) whose two Bs indicate that it was made at the Bute Workshops in the 1890s

Below: The Cross-House

The centre panel on this 17th-century chest in the King's Room depicts a woman holding a shield bearing the lion of Scotland. The panels on either side contain fierce masks of satyrs

RENAISSANCE SANITATION

Three latrine drains were found in the palace during Lord Bute's excavations, the middle one linked to a pipe system descending from a closet room. Prior to the reign of James V, latrines (for those of higher birth – the servants had to relieve themselves outdoors) usually took the form of a fixed seat in a cubicle contained in the thickness of a castle wall or in a projecting turret. Beneath the seat was a stone-built chute down which the effluent descended to a pit or cistern at the base of the wall. At Falkland, running water flushed these pits. Even when regularly cleaned and kept fresh with sweet-smelling herbs, these latrines would have been unpleasant, and in the 16th century the 'stool of ease' was introduced for the king and selected members of his household. This contained a bowl that was emptied by an unfortunate servant after use.

The 3rd Marquess and his architect John Kinross recreated the fabric of the Cross-House following the available evidence, but the work was not completed by 1900, when the Marquess died. Together with the National Trust for Scotland, Michael Crichton Stuart realised his grandfather's intentions for the creation here of two rooms which would evoke the history of this part of the palace. The architect for this work was W Schomberg Scott. A Scottish artist, David McClure, painted the royal monograms within the compartments of the wooden ceiling, the frieze around the tops of the walls and, over the fireplace, the royal arms of James V, taken from a contemporary portrait of the king.

The room contains several notable pieces of furniture. The most obvious is the Golden Bed of Brahan, which was made in the Dutch East Indies in the early 17th century, richly carved by craftsmen who were either Dutch or strongly influenced by Dutch work. The bed was brought to Scotland by Daniel Mackenzie, and given by him to the 2nd Earl of Seaforth, who kept it at Brahan Castle in Ross & Cromarty, now demolished. It was gifted to the National Trust for Scotland by the Seaforth family.

The Stuart monarchs sometimes took their beds with them when the court moved between palaces. The royal accounts record that in May 1539 three carriages were needed to take 'the king's great green bed' from Falkland to St Andrews. The royal beds, like the one in this room, were elaborately hung with velvet, taffeta, silk and damask.

The king's privy chamber was serviced by grooms, who made up the fires, cleared away the mattresses on which the chamber staff slept, and cleaned the chamber, all before their master rose. The king would bathe – probably not very often – in a wooden tub in the closet off his chamber, hot water having been brought up from the kitchen by servants. The tub was usually lined with cloth and draped with a canopy to give him some privacy. The hole in the corner of the closet was originally used as a latrine, but later probably for tipping away the used bathwater.

Above the entrance doorway is a copy of the death mask of Mary, Queen of Scots, setting the tone for the room, which has been arranged to suggest that this might have been hers. It was furnished in 1987 to mark the 400th anniversary of Mary's execution. Her royal arms are depicted over the fireplace, and a niche to the left of the bed, containing an oval embroidery of the Annunciation, represents a small oratory for private prayer.

The room is notable for its curved wooden barrel-vaulted ceiling, and for its fine furniture – the tall cupboard and bed from the Bute Workshops, and a 17th-century chest and chairs.

CARING FOR THE COLLECTIONS

Preventive conservation is particularly important at Falkland Palace given the importance and sensitive nature of the objects here. The Trust makes every effort to prevent damage to the collection, by installing environmental monitoring systems to record the relative humidity, temperature and light levels in the rooms. We then analyse this data to create a stable environment. Good housekeeping also keeps control of the level of dust, without over-cleaning, which can be potentially damaging.

In the Tapestry Gallery, we regularly check and photograph the tapestries, carefully monitoring any deterioration of the fibres and assessing when remedial conservation may be required to prevent loss of the original fabric. Light is a main cause of damage to the tapestries and to other objects in the collection, so we have installed blinds to control light levels, as well as a special film applied to the window glass to limit the harmful ultraviolet light entering the rooms.

Sometimes we need to contract highly qualified conservators to provide specialist skills. Conservation has been carried out on the wall paintings in the Keeper's Drawing Room and the Keeper's Dressing Room, maintaining and preserving the 1890s decoration. This is a long-term project that demands close monitoring of the environment and the condition of the paint to determine the exact causes of damage and therefore the most appropriate solution.

OUTSIDE THE PALACE

THE REAL TENNIS COURT

The Real (or Royal) Tennis Court was built in 1539 for James V and is the oldest in Britain. Unlike the courts at the Palace of Holyroodhouse, Edinburgh, and Linlithgow Palace, it never had a roof. Originally, the internal walls were painted black. The attached building on the west side may have been added later in the 16th century: it could have been a stable or a bowling alley.

The four walls of the court and the viewing area are all part of the playing area. When the king played doubles on the court, six people took part – the king, his partner and a servant on one side, two opponents and a servant on the other. The servant served the ball for the king and then retired from play.

The young Mary, Queen of Scots, James V's daughter, is said to have shocked her courtiers by donning breeches to play here.

THE RULES OF THE GAME

A contemporary drawing of a tennis game in Padua in 1610

Originally known as 'cachpull', the game of royal tennis resembled a cross between modern lawn tennis and squash but, unlike them, demanded skill and subtlety more than speed and strength. It had evolved from the medieval 'jeu de paume' ('game of the palm of the hand') whose popularity had swept through France and northern Europe. Royal tennis could be played with an asymmetric racket as well as with the hand, and the ball was heavy and solid.

The server – always starting the game from the same end of the court – hit the ball over a tasselled rope stretched across the centre of the court. The ball had to bounce on the side penthouse roof before dropping within the red-lined service area. If it hit the 'ais' (the wooden stave at the bottom right-hand corner of the court), or went through one of the 'lunes' (holes in the opposite wall), the server won an outright point.

If the opposite player failed to return the ball after one bounce, they did not necessarily lose a point, and the final score depended also on the winning of 'chases' (hitting the ball into prescribed areas of the court).

This court is still used regularly by a local group, the Falkland Palace Real Tennis Club.

THE GARDEN

The garden at Falkland Palace starts to bloom in early May, when the blossoms of cherry and apple trees in the orchard create a spectacular spring display (opposite page). Then in summer the garden fills with colour and fragrance from the dramatic herbaceous perennials (above). It continues to give pleasure well into autumn, with late flowering phlox and the vibrant red colours of the paper-bark maple and Sorbus commixta *(below)*

The palace stands in three hectares of grounds; it is built on a sandstone ridge and dominates the rich agricultural plain. From the main garden, which is enclosed by high walls, there are extensive views of the hills to the north, and of the woodland that has replaced the medieval forest where the Stuart monarchs hunted wild boar and deer. The garden is exposed to the cold north-easterly winds that sweep across the Howe of Fife; its soil is neutral and drains naturally.

The first record of a garden here dates from 1451, the year James II began work on the palace. The Exchequer Rolls record the payment of a gardener's salary, which is repeated in 1453 and 1456, with a note that the salary was undeserved: the gardener was later dismissed. In 1484, instructions were recorded not to pay the gardener unless he worked well; in response, he produced eight barrels of onions for the king's use, and this, gradually reduced to four barrels, became an annual form of reddendo (the service or payment due from a vassal to his superior). Working hours in the garden in the early 16th century ranged from 8 a day in winter to 14 in summer. The working week was six days, but there were no fewer than 45 holidays a year – mostly saints' days and religious festivals.

We also know from records that in 1462 a lawn was created that could be reached by a staircase from the room now known as the Queen's Room. By 1488 the garden was enclosed with a wooden fence, which was replaced by a stone wall in 1513.

The royal stables were rebuilt around 1530, replacing stables built within the gates in 1461, where King James IV kept his great Belgian horse, probably used for transporting the royal goods and chattels. To the west of the stables was a stank or fishpond to provide the royal kitchen with fresh fish.

This 1640 painting of Falkland by Alexander Keirincx shows the palace garden with its double walled enclosure

A detail of a Falkland estate plan of c1830, 'the property of Onesiphorus Tyndall Bruce Esquire'

In 1628 James VI's son Charles I is recorded as 'planting and contriving the garden anew', with sundials and pillars, at considerable cost. Almost two centuries later, during John Bruce's ownership of the Falkland estate, a kitchen garden was laid out in the general area of the present water garden, with fruit trees trained against the walls of the tennis court. In the 'lower ground' – the area north and south of the present water garden, delineated by the east range of the palace, the tennis court and the east boundary wall – fruit trees were planted and thorn bushes were established, then transplanted out as hedges around the improved field system on the Falkland estate. The 'upper ground' at the level of the palace courtyard included the area around the foundations of the old castle, which were sloped and levelled by Bruce in 1822.

From 1826 to 1869 the kitchen/fruit/flower garden developed further under Onesiphorus and Margaret Tyndall Bruce: the records reveal glasshouses, a vinery, a peach house, and pineapple and melon pits (none of which remain). Some of this work may be attributable to John Bruce, but the Tyndall Bruces were almost certainly responsible for the Regency-style garden laid out in the palace courtyard (now the Keeper's Lawn). This garden was sketched by Onesiphorus in 1841: but it does not appear on the first OS map of 1854, having been superseded by a more formal layout.

As part of his restoration of the palace in the 1890s, the 3rd Marquess of Bute enhanced the ornamental kitchen garden with a pergola and decorative vases, and replanted the orchard. The north part of the 'upper ground' was reshaped to accommodate the foundations of Falkland Castle and the north range of the palace, which were uncovered during Bute's archaeological excavations. He linked the orchard and palace gardens to the House of Falkland by a private walk with bridges, which still exists. The ground around the curling pond was planted with trees and shrubs and laid out in flower plots.

This area is now a woodland garden planted with British ferns and cultivars, featuring *Polypodium*, *Athyrium* and *Polystichum*. A living sculpture – *Lady of the Wood* – has been planted with Irish and Scottish moss and acts as a focal point.

The main garden to the east was dug as a forest nursery during the First World War and for the cultivation of potatoes during the Second World War in the 'Dig for Victory' campaign.

The courtyard garden: an engraving of 1841

This photograph of 1879 records the now vanished monument by Sir John Steell that was erected in the palace courtyard in 1865. It commemorated Margaret Bruce's uncle, Professor John Bruce, and her father Colonel Robert Bruce. The iron from the monument was donated to the war effort in the 1940s, but some of the stonework is still stored in the stable block

Barbara Crichton Stuart and Bill Jenkin in the garden

'A LITTLE MAN WITH VISION': PERCY CANE

Percy Cane (1881–1976) was an artist, horticultural writer and garden designer. He was born and educated in Essex, studying both horticulture and architecture. He founded and edited the influential quarterly journal *Garden Design* in 1930 and wrote many books on garden design.

In addition to here at Falkland Palace, his garden designs can still be seen all over Britain. Perhaps his most illustrious commission was the design of the palace gardens at Addis Ababa, commissioned by Emperor Haile Selassie of Ethiopia. Some of the characteristic features of his Arts & Crafts style, such as the curved borders, were innovatory in the 1930s. 'He had vision, that little man,' commented Barbara Crichton Stuart of Cane.

John Slezer's 1693 engraving of Falkland

Major Michael Crichton Stuart and his wife Barbara advertised for a gardener soon after they took over the Keepership of the palace in 1946. Barbara recorded: 'We had 97 replies ... The first one we saw was Jenkin, and we took him. I couldn't resist his Cheshire-cat smile.' W J (Bill) Jenkin was a Cornishman who had been trained in the gardens at Tresco. He stayed here until 1975, during which time he created the rose garden in the completely ruined north range, which had been laid out following and emphasising the lines of the newly excavated foundations. From 1961 he was helped by his son Jimmy, of whom Michael Crichton Stuart commented at first: 'He is a good enough lad … Whether he'll stick to the job remains to be seen.' In fact, he stayed at Falkland for 43 years, retiring in 2003.

The most important initiative of the Crichton Stuarts was to invite the celebrated garden designer Percy Cane to recreate the gardens at Falkland Palace between 1947 and 1952. Cane's design for what he termed 'the pleasure grounds' at Falkland was influenced by John Slezer's 1693 engraving of Falkland from the east, which emphasised the impressive views of the surrounding hills (see top of page). To maintain this outlook from the garden, Cane created a central glade enclosed by six large island beds, and a grass walk meandering around the terrace between the straight edges of the outer borders and curving lines of the inner islands.

Cane planted many trees in the garden – chiefly fern leaved beech and Norway maple 'Crimson King', which strikingly complemented the copper beech and oak circle planted in 1887 by the 3rd Marquess of Bute. He also designed the main garden to the east of the oak circle, with its long lawn, specimen trees and swelling half-moon beds. The beds are planted in layers, with small trees like cherries and maples in the middle, descending to shrubs such as *Deutzia*, *Weigela* and *Philadelphus*; these are surrounded by smaller plants such as *Potentilla*, hostas, *Erigeron* and other groundcovers. Most impressive is the vast herbaceous border which extends the full length of the eastern perimeter wall – 180 by 5.4 metres. It is planted with a succession of flowers, with a central block of reds, yellows and oranges: the border is at its spectacular best between July and September.

The unbroken extent of this border, which gives it such impact, was not intended by Cane, according to Barbara Crichton Stuart. He had planned a recess, but Jenkin had other ideas. 'Dear Jenkin,' Barbara recalled. 'He was marvellous, a tremendous worker, but very opinionated. The first time Percy Cane called out "Gardener!" you could see Jenkin squirm. If you told him to do something he was inclined to do the opposite.'

The inner bed, below the ruined east range of the palace and the old castle site, was planted by Cane with large blocks of bearded irises and Russell lupins – hybrids introduced in 1937 by George Russell. By 1988, the lupins had declined and, following a suggestion made by Cane in 1964, were replaced by 320 Pacific hybrid delphiniums.

The magnificent herbaceous
border. By the late 1980s
the lupins planted here by
Percy Cane (below) had been
replaced with delphiniums (left)

Cane built steps to link the old castle foundations and the well garden with the glade and midway between the two, perched on top of the garden wall beneath the towering rampart of the east range, he laid out a long paved walk as a vantage point from which to survey the whole scene. The rest of this higher ground has been left as a lawn: at its summit five old oaks form a ring. Closer to the palace stands a small *Acer pseudoplatanus* 'Worleei', a replacement of the one planted by the Queen Mother in 1981 to celebrate the Golden Jubilee of the Trust.

The terraces were redesigned by Cane to be 'unvarying green' and the ruined north range enclosing the courtyard was marked by a formal paved flower garden. The old Great Hall, excavated by Lord Bute, is now being planted in the style of a Renaissance physic garden, based on *Gerard's Herbal* (1597). It features a variety of medicinal and culinary herbs including lavender, rosemary, thyme, oregano and winter savory. Mary, Queen of Scots would have been familiar with this type of garden.

In 1955 the water garden was created beside the Real Tennis Court, with two raised water basins complete with waterlilies. 'The pools have lilies and should have goldfish, but this ruddy heron comes and scoops them all up,' wrote Barbara Crichton Stuart. Two large urns planted with *Vitis coignetiae* preside over the entrance to the garden, which is almost totally enclosed by yew hedges. The only gap gives one of the most superb views back up to the east garden.

The glasshouse, south of the water garden, was designed in 1890 by Mackenzie and Moncur of Edinburgh and reconstructed in 1985. It is home to the most comprehensive collection of pelargoniums in Scotland, with more than 180 different species and cultivars that include the superb red 'Mrs Morris', planted by Jenkin in 1948

Opposite page: the water garden.

43

In 1952 Major Crichton Stuart and his wife arranged for the National Trust for Scotland to become Deputy Keeper of the palace. 'We gave [the orchard] to the National Trust as well,' Barbara Crichton Stuart commented, 'to stop anyone building bungalows there if we all went under a bus.' Percy Cane wrote that 'the gardens at Falkland must be unique in the United Kingdom as having been restored by an individual at considerable expense and almost immediately handed over to the Trust for public benefit.'

In 1965, to meet the increase in visitors, a Visitor Centre designed by W Schomberg Scott was built at the south end where the garden adjoins the main street. Today, this building houses the palace's gift shop. He also designed the flagged courtyard on two levels ornamented with lavender, a three-foot stone owl and an immense stone draughtsboard with black and red draughts. To the south-east is an armillary sphere commemorating Major Michael and Barbara Crichton Stuart.

The Trust continues to manage the garden – one of Percy Cane's most complete designs – in accordance with his principles, retaining the balance and scale of the original plantings. The garden is widely acknowledged as outstanding both for its historical value and as a work of art.

WILDLIFE INHABITANTS AND VISITORS

Pellitory of the wall, seldom seen in Scotland except on old historic walls like those at Falkland, was used to cure urinary ailments

Below: Red squirrel

Below right: Soprano pipistrelle

The old palace walls, gardens and grounds are a haven for a wide variety of wildlife. The mortar and spaces in the old walls nurture many ferns, such as the brittle bladder fern, wall rue, and the lacy fronds of the lady fern. Unimproved turf on top of the old garden walls supports many grassland plants that have disappeared elsewhere in the countryside, such as the lovely lemon-yellow flowers of the mouse-ear hawkweed, the ox-eye daisy and the locally rare white ramping fumitory. Their colour is enhanced by the purples of selfheal and bush vetch and the bright blue of germander speedwell, growing in or beside the lawns and attracting bumblebees to the garden.

Butterflies such as the meadow brown, small tortoiseshell and peacock commonly flit around the flower borders and the orchard, whilst keen-eyed visitors may spot the rare purple hairstreak butterfly flying around the tops of the oak trees. The ponds beside the Real Tennis Court hold a fascinating array of wildlife and there is always something going on within their waters as mayfly nymphs and newt larvae avoid the hungry mouths of damselfly larvae.

The newly established wildflower meadow around the orchard is now full of wild flowers, including abundant yellow rattle and viper's bugloss, making it an uplifting place for a gentle stroll. Recent research by experts has shown that these meadows are home to over 40 species of fly alone, including some Scottish rarities, already showing that the sensitive management of this area is reaping benefits for wildlife.

No visitor to Falkland can miss the swallows that breed here, notably in the Real Tennis Court, and the swifts that 'scream' above the gardens. The song thrush, with its beautiful song, also lives and breeds in the grounds, and the tranquil orchard attracts greenfinch and bullfinch. The palace gardens are one of the increasingly rare places in Fife where you can see red squirrels, and we hope their return to the grounds will go from strength to strength.

At night, bats feed in the grounds: soprano pipistrelles and the rarer Natterer's bat devour the moths attracted by the garden shrubs and flowers. They use the palace's cellars to roost during the day.

The Trust carries out continuous wildlife surveys and monitoring work at Falkland Palace to ensure we conserve key wildlife interests. As part of this, we encourage visitors to tell us about any wildlife they see on the property.

In 1458 Falkland was made into a Royal Burgh, reflecting the status of the palace rather than of the village itself. At the west end are the entrance gates to the House of Falkland, leading into a fine designed landscape, restored between 2003 and 2006 with the assistance of the Heritage Lottery Fund. Information is available at the Falkland Heritage Trust in the Stables. The house is now a school, and open to the public only for special events.

Margaret and Onesiphorus Tyndall Bruce commissioned William Burn (1789–1870) to design a new House of Falkland. It was built between 1839 and 1844, and is one of his best surviving Jacobean-style country houses. A formal garden and pleasure grounds were designed by the Italian-born Alexander Roos (1810–81), who was also responsible for the burgh's drinking fountain, and for forest planting and embellishments on the Lomond Hills, including the Temple of Decision, currently awaiting restoration. David Bryce, another outstanding mid-19th-century architect, was commissioned by the Tyndall Bruces to design a new parish church (1848–50). He also designed, to the east of the church, the plinth on which stands the bronze statue of Onesiphorus by Sir John Steell.

Top: the House of Falkland (right) and the bridge in its designed landscape. Centre: the parish church and the monumental fountain

*Right: St Andrew's House,
one of the Trust's self-catering
holiday properties*

The Town Hall, opposite the palace, was built in 1800–01. The town council met here until local government reorganisation in 1975. The building was purchased by the National Trust for Scotland in 1986 and now contains an exhibition about the Royal Burgh.

South and west of the High Street is a tightly knit huddle of streets where a dozen cottages bear distinctive small plaques indicating that the National Trust for Scotland repaired the building and sold it on with agreements for its future preservation, through its Little Houses Improvement Scheme.

Further to the south, where the ground begins to rise up to the Lomond Hills, is the site of the former Linoleum Works of 1931 designed by C H Armour, which went on to manufacture paper bags. This image shows the factory before it was demolished in 2017, as the site is now earmarked for residential development.

*A cottage in High Street West
in 1960 before restoration
and today*